THE
signerika

MARK TO BE BORNE

BY LARK AAKARSHAN

IDEA | 01. 02. | WHAT IT IS AND NOT

ME | 03. 04. | YOU

A B C D E F

G H I J K L M

N O P Q R S T

U V W X Y Z

HOW ONE PERCEIVES?
SYMBOLS AND SHAPES?
OUR BRAIN
IS AN INSTRUMENT THAT
PERCEIVE FORMS
NOT PARTIALLY BUT AS A WHOLE
NOT AS IT VIEW THINGS
BUT CREATES ASSOCIATION OF THEM
WITH PREVIOUSLY UNDERSTOOD
IDEAS AND COGNITIONS

THE CONCEPT IS
TO TRANSLATE THE IDEAS
INTO SYMBOLS
WHERE LIES A DEEPER MEANING
TO BE DECODED AND MOULDED
INTO IDEAS OF PERCEPTION
THE DEMONSTRATED FORMS
INVITE THE USER TO INTERACT
AND IMPLY THEIR OWN JUSTIFICATIONS FOR EACH
HELPING THEM BROADEN
THE SCOPE OF THEIR
UNDERSTANDING AND DEVELPOMENT

THIS IS NOT

a rule book. It invites you
to construct your own rule
and put forward your
own justification

the collection of logos or
symbols but a guide to
demonstrate how simple
forms can be made to
manifest into deeper
interpretations

a logo or branding guide
but an insight to invite
deeper thinking

Œ ɜ Æ

a tool to deepen
within the user a
scope to find hidden
meanings around

THIS
IS

the compilation of ideas
enlivened as forms

a manual of aiding one to
create logos, mascots,
symbols, notions, icons,
infographics, emblems or
to say an expression of
art to be kept framed

IT IS YOU
WHO DEFINES
THE RULES

If you have a strong validation to justify t h e m	If you can make others understand and respond	If you can generate curiosity to be n o t i c e d

Throughout this journey you
will be made to interact with
different ideas developed
and converted to enliven as a
form to make you look
beyond the ordinary; to
perceive by deeper explora-
tions and understanding

There are no values or ways
of being something right or
w   r   o   n   g

But it is you who defines
with your own verdict, justi-
fications, validation and
e x p l a n a t i o n s

NOTHING
DEFINES THE
RIGHT OR
WRONG
PRACTICE BUT
YOUR OWN
VERDICT AND
SCOPE OF
VALIDATION

OUR WORLD IS NOT
LIMITED
TO OUR
CONSCIOUSNESS
BUT FAR DEEPER
LIES OUR
SUB CONCIOUS
WHERE
THE ACTUAL
"MAGIC"
HAPPENS

SUBCONCIOUS

IS 10000 X
MORE POWERFUL
THAN CONCIOUS
& WORKS
WITHOUT ANY
OBSTACLES OR
JUDGEMENT
BECAUSE
IT DOES'NT
QUESTIONS

BUT ONLY
ACTS
ON WHATEVER
WE MAKE IT
PROCESS

OUR
SUBCONCIOUS
DOES'NT
UNDERSTANTD
ANY LANGUAGE
NEITHER
HINDI
ENGLISH
ARABIC
SANSKRIT
SPANISH
HERBREW

WHAT IT UNDERSTANDS IS

SIGNS

SYMBOLS

ONCE THE
INFORMATION
IS CONVERTED INTO SPECIFIC
GLYPHS
IT BECOMES
EASIER FOR
SUBCONCIOUS
TO PROCESS

AND THEN OUR
DESIRES
TURN INTO
REALITIES

ITS MY DESIRE
TO BE
FAMOUS

ITS MY DESIRE
TO BE
ELEGANT

ITS MY DESIRE
TO BE
ARTISTIC

ITS MY DESIRE
TO BE
JOVIAL

I WANT TO
EXPERIENCE
HAPPINESS
IN MY LIFE

I WANT TO
EXPERIENCE
EUPHORIA
IN MY LIFE

I WANT TO
EXPERIENCE
REJUVENATION
IN MY LIFE

I WANT TO
EXPERIENCE
WISDOM
IN MY LIFE

This book is evolved from the old occult rituals where desires are transformed into symbols later on fueling the energy in those developed forms making them enliven. The most aspirated desires are shortlisted and converted into forms, arranged alpha-betically; can be observed throughout this manual

★
THE SIGIL
IS THE CONCEPT OF
TRANSLATING
THE DESIRES INTO
GLYPHS
WHICH CAN BE MADE TO PROCESS BY OUR
SUBCONCIOUSNESS
MAKING THEM TURN INTO
REALITIES
★ ★ ★

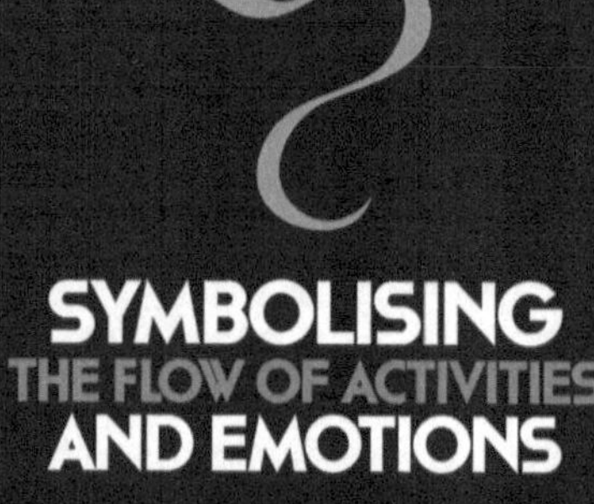
SYMBOLISING
THE FLOW OF ACTIVITIES
AND EMOTIONS

+

SYMBOLISING
THE TERMIANL POINTS
DIRECTING THE FLOW

mesmerized by the feeling to
enlive the freedom of joy and
hope with the sense of
begining and end

with the animated life of vigor
and spirit suspended as tapestry
in the midst of the wind

SYMBOLISING
THE CONCENTRATED
RESOURCES WITHIN

+

SYMBOLISING
THE DISPERSION
OF RESOURCES

ALTRUISM

UNSELFISH DISPERSION OF ONESELF FOR OTHERS

the behaviour comprising
concern for the well
being of others

the distribution of centric
resources within oneself
amongst the adiding

SYMBOLISING
THE FREE FLOWING PASSION
FOR CREATIVITY

SYMBOLISING
THE TENDENCY FOR
INQUISITIVENESS

★ ARTISTIC

FLOWING FREE WITH INQUISITIVE CREATIVITY

living life with the blend of
creative freedom and expression
with the tendancy to discover
new and experiment

★ ★ ★

when the mind tends to be the
part of the spirit to float
anonymously reaching the places
never discovered previously in
an endless fashion of
self amusement

—————— ★ ★ ★ ——————

SYMBOLISING
THE UNLIMITED
STRENGTH AND POWER

SYMBOLISING
THE RADIATING
ESSENCE OF ULTIMATE

ABUNDANT
EXISTING INFINITELY IN AMPLE PROFUSION

ready for dispersion without the
fear of loosing being the rich
source of power

shining in all its might with the
rich and plentiful acquirement
of one's inner being

SYMBOLISING
THE CONCISTENCY OF
PROGRESS

SYMBOLISING
THE ACHIEVEMENT
OF VICTORY

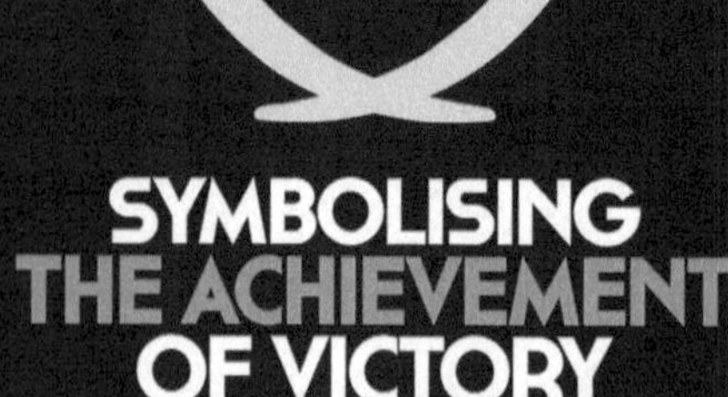

gradual development of ability
towards success creating one to
become a winner

★ ★ ★

step by step development making
one richer on each stage in
acquiring the ability

SYMBOLISING THE ACTION

+

SYMBOLISING THE POSITIVE
POTENTIAL TO ENACT

the act consisting of
the positive notification of the
action to occur or happen

the energy directy in a particular
direction to make an event occur

SYMBOLISING
ONE ATTRIBUTE

SYMBOLISING
ANOTHER ATTRIBUTE

considering all arguments,
opinions, or aspects fairly
and equally

showing the perfect symmetry in
its form and constituents with no
tendency towards favoritism

SYMBOLISING
THE INWARD FLOW OF
EXCELLENCE AND KNOWLEDGE

+

SYMBOLISING
THE OUTER
DISPERSION OF ACQUIRED

BRILLIANCE
SHINING UNLIKE ANYTHING

the disposition of great skill
or intelligence

dispersing intense brightness
and light

SYMBOLISING
DIVERSE MOVEMENT

SYMBOLISING
THE OPEN ENDED
FLOW

BOUNDLESS
FREE FROM RESTRICTIONS AND ENDS

bounded yet free to flow
immensely as if there exists no
barriers bounding its motion

★ ★ ★

experiencing unlimted power free
from boundations in the motion
of freedom

★ ★ ★

SYMBOLISING
THE FORCE OF
ATTRIBUTES

+

**SYMBOLISING
THE INTERCEPTED**
UNION OF ATTRIBUTES

COMPLETE
FROM THE MIND, BODY AND HEART

one tends to deliver and achieve
totality with the existence of
union of distinct attributes of
mind, body and heart

★ ★ ★

consisiting of all the
necessary elements

SYMBOLISING
THE BROKEN GAP

SYMBOLISING
MENDING OVER

COMPASSION
THE EXPRESSION OF AIDING THE BROKEN

delivreance of mercy for the
sufferings and misfortunes
of others

mending one the broken
suffering from unfortunate
contingencies

SYMBOLISING
THE CONCENTRATED
STRENGTH AND POWER

+

SYMBOLISING
THE BALANCE OF
AUTHORITY AND PERFECTION

DIVINE
THE PERFECTION BEYOND THE BALANCE

the feeling of upliftment beyond
ones comfort zone, circle with
the prime association of infinity
raised over the balance

the sun is the resemblance of the
perfection mounted static
crowned denoting the power of
supremacy raised higher never
deviated from its balnce

SYMBOLISING
THE UNIQUENESS
STANDING OUT

+

SYMBOLISING
THE CLUSTERED
WORLD OF CROWD

recognizably different in nature
from something else

noticed out easily amongst the
crowd with distinct tast of
opacity and boldness

SYMBOLISING
THE SPEED OF STRIKE
OF LIGHTNING

**SYMBOLISING
FULCRUM FOR
ROTATION**

DYNAMIC

WHIRLING AT A PACE OF LIGHTINING

striking in its act with
consistent change difficult
to place at halt

★ ★ ★

tendency to work with efficiency
throughout the span

★ ★ ★

SYMBOLISING
THE CONFINEMENT
OF RATIONALITY

+

SYMBOLISING
THE OPPOSITION

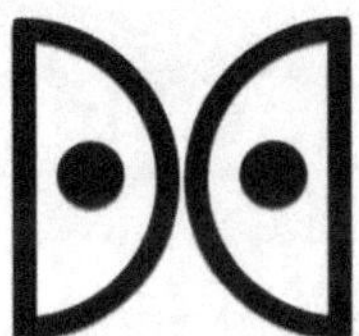

opposing emotions
demonstrating the ability of
rational decision making

★ ★ ★

two halves pointing in opposite
direction as opposing each
other, the emotions with the bold
dots denoting rationalisation

SYMBOLISING
THE ABILITY OF BEING
AT BOTH THE ENDS

+

SYMBOLISING
THE BINDING
OF BOTH THE ENDS

DIPLOMATIC
IDEA OF TACKLING BY DUAL FAVORITISM

idea of answering in a manner
defending both the parties as
of killing two birds with
a single stone

with the twin circles denoting
two parties and the answer acting
as a bigger circle favouring in
both of the parties so to avoid
any confliction raised

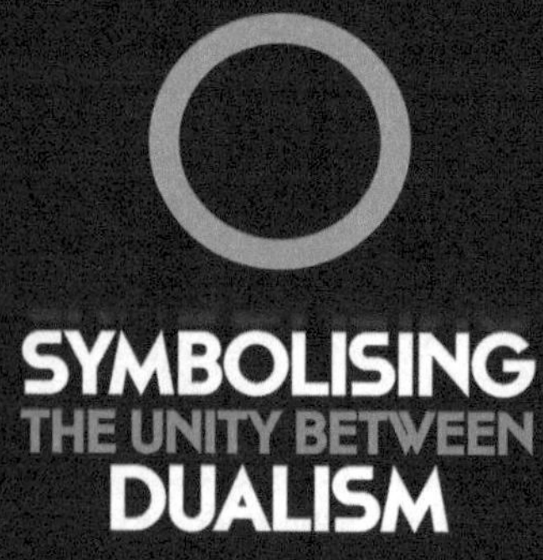

SYMBOLISING
DUAL HANDED
SET OF SKILLS DIRECTED

DEXTERITY
DUAL HANDED SKILLED PERFORMANCE

dual hands binded together
directed for the achievement of a
particular task

skill in performing tasks
with hands

SYMBOLISING
THE ACT OF STRENGTHENED
TO THE GROUND

SYMBOLISING
THE SUCCESS

DETERMINATION
GROUNDED WITH STRONG BELIEFS TO SUCCEED

the process of establishing
strong belief towards
achievement

the process of controlling
what something will be by
grounding one's position

SYMBOLISING
THE ONE HALF

+

SYMBOLISING
THE OTHER HALF

EQUALITY

equal blends of both the halves

★ ★ ★

the condition of being equal in
number or amount

SYMBOLISING
A RADIATING STAR

SYMBOLISING
A STRENGTHENED
STAND

EMINENT
STANDOUT LIKE A STAR SHINING

emphasized with a quality of
standing out from rest

famous and respected with a
particular quality

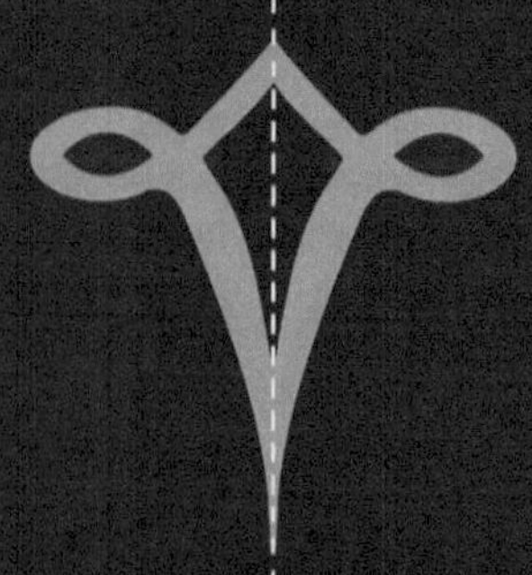

SYMBOLISING
THE FEMININE
ATTRIBUTE OF ELEGANCE
WITH BALNCE OF
SYMMETRY

ENCHANTING

THE EXPRESSION OF PERFECTION EVER NOTICEABLE

Delightfully charming and
attractive, emphasising over
the feminine aspect in the
form of female ovaries

★ ★ ★

capturing interest as if
by a spell

SYMBOLISING
THE SIMILAR OTHERS

SYMBOLISING
THE BOLDER

EXCLUSIVE

RARE OCCURENCE NOTICEABLE AMONGST ALIKE

standing out amongst others

the attribute of great value
uniquely possessed by one not
necessarily the centre of
attention but inhibit the charac-
terstic no one else consists

SYMBOLISING
THE INCOMPLETE YET
TO PROGRESS

+

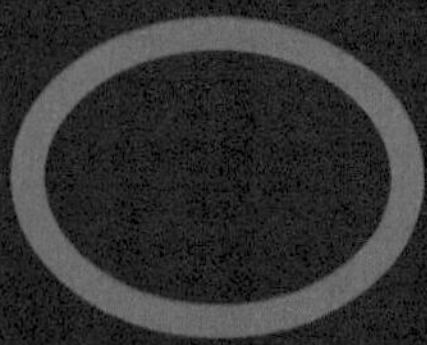

**SYMBOLISING
THE DEVELOPMENT**

the origin of life stated to water
developing from fishes to humans

the systematic development by
facilitating comparison between
where we were and where we are

SYMBOLISING
THE FOURCES OF
PRESSURE

SYMBOLISING
SPRINGY DURABILITY

ENDURANCE
THE DURABILITY TO WITHSTAND PRESSURE

the ability to withstand extensive
force without getting harmed

★ ★ ★

the power of enduring an
unpleasant or difficult process or
situation without giving way

SYMBOLISING
THE COMFORT
FROM ALL SIDES

SYMBOLISING
THE SPIRITUAL
SPARK OF UNDERSTANDING

ENLIGHTENMENT
COMFORT ACQUIRED FROM SPIRITUAL UNDERSTANDING

feeling the comfort inside of
being stable and peaceful with
the attainment of spiritual
understanding getting imbibed
deep inide oneself

★ ★ ★

phenomenon of attainment
of spiritual knowledge or insight

SYMBOLISING
THE FLUIDITY

+

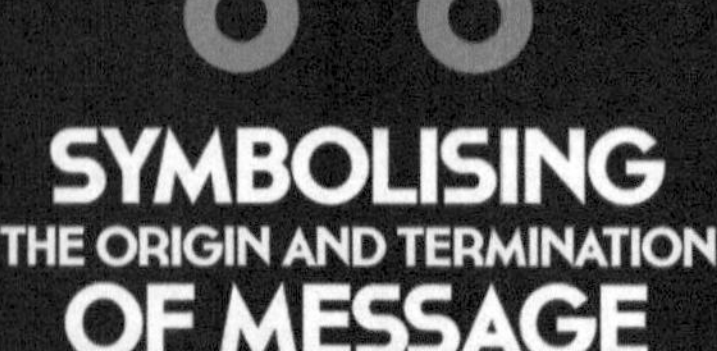

SYMBOLISING
THE ORIGIN AND TERMINATION
OF MESSAGE

FLUENT

FLUID COMMUNICATION OF AN EXPRESSION

the efficient flow in the delivery
of a message from initial
to terminal

expressing oneself easily
and articulately

SYMBOLISING THE CANVAS

+

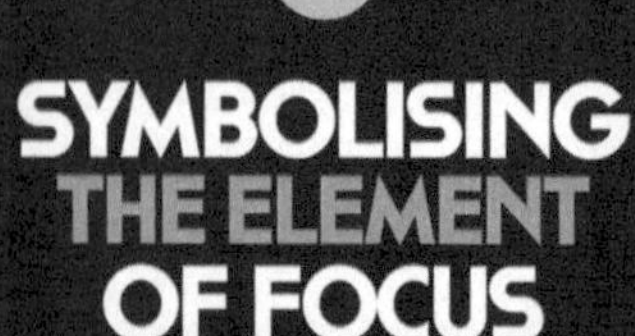

SYMBOLISING THE ELEMENT OF FOCUS

FOCUSED
THE CONCENTRATED PERCEPTION

concentrating the view over the
specific in the field

uninterrupted attention afixed
over particular

SYMBOLISING
THE CONCENTRATED
STRENGTH AND POWER

+

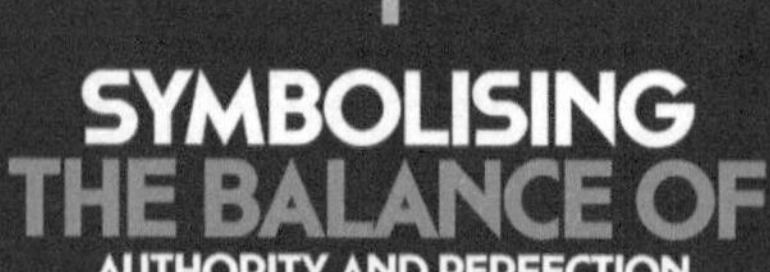

SYMBOLISING
THE BALANCE OF
AUTHORITY AND PERFECTION

FRESH

RISING WITH NEW ASPIRATIONS

the feeling of upliftment beyond
ones comfort zone. the circle
with the prime association of
infinity raised over the balance of

the sun is the resemblance of the
perfection mounted static
crowned denoting the power of
supremacy. Bound by excelence
and infinte existencve it
is never deviated

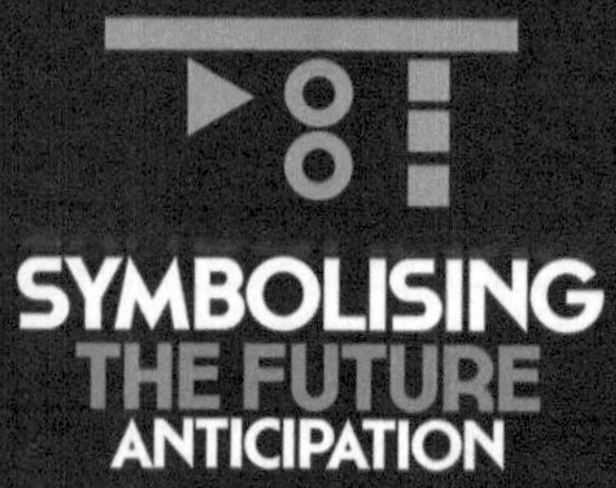

SYMBOLISING
THE FUTURE
ANTICIPATION

SYMBOLISING
THE FUTURE

FUTURISTIC
PLANNING MAPPING THE FUTURE

anticipating the future values and
planning present accordingly
in a similar fashion

★ ★ ★

characterised by the skill to
seek for future

SYMBOLISING
THE REMEBERED
SOLUTION

SYMBOLISING
THE FORGOTTEN
STATE

FORGIVE
DELIBERATE ACT OF FORGETTING TO JOIN

the act of deliberately forgetting
that something occured
by a culprit

a way to potray out the feeling of
forgetting of non occurence of
the event by someone which
happened at some point.

SYMBOLISING
A FLOWER

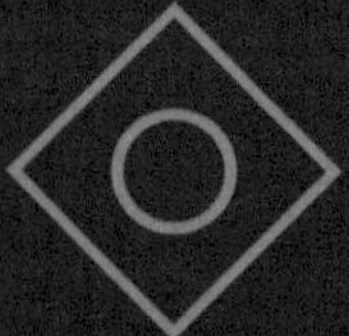
SYMBOLISING
A CONTAINER

FLAMBOYANT
MARKED BY ITS AESTHETIC & DELECATE APPEAL

with its aesthetic symettrical
balance inviting others to get
noticed blooming emanating
out from its container

tending to attract attention
because of their exuberance,
confidence, and stylishness

SYMBOLISING
THE ORDINARY
BEHIND THE WALLS

\+

SYMBOLISING
THE ONE TO
BE AFRONT

FORTUNATE
CHANCE FAVOURED AGAINST ONE

the one favoured by luck tends to
showcase infront while the others
stay behind the secnes

the successful movement of one
among others staying behind

SYMBOLISING
THE INCREMENT

+

SYMBOLISING
THE ALL ROUND

GROWTH
THE OVERALL PHENOMENON

the desirous phenomenon of
mental, physical, spiritual and
increment in all phases of life

★ ★ ★

being the multilateral concept
rather than unilateral

SYMBOLISING
THE VICTORIOUS WEAPON

+

SYMBOLISING
THE GLOWING
CANDLESTAND

GLORIOUS
STANDING OUT WITH ILLUMINATION

shining out with all its victory
with the winning battle

the striking beauty and splendor
that evokes feelings of delighted
admiration

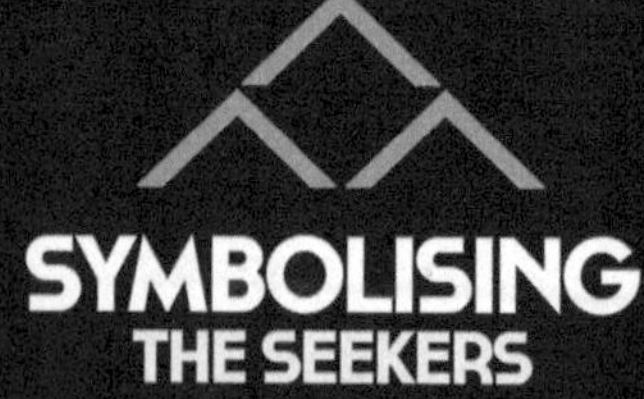
SYMBOLISING
THE SEEKERS

+

SYMBOLISING
THE GUIDE
HEADING TOWARDS SUCCESS

a force directing the seekers
towards the attainment
of success

directing of the motion or
position of something

SYMBOLISING
THE ORIGINALITY

GENUINE
CLEAR IN ITS REPRESENTATION

clear and original in its approach
showcasing no flourishes
or extravagance

Truly what something is
said to be

SYMBOLISING
THE HEAVENLY ABODE

+

SYMBOLISING
THE DIFFERENT PLANES
OF EXISTENCE

beyond the all known planes
of existence

supernal and divine of the sky

SYMBOLISING
THE HORIZION BASE
+

SYMBOLISING
THE NEW RISE

HOPE
AN EXPECTATION TO RISE

a feeling of expectation and
desire for a certain thing
to happen or occur

★ ★ ★

the anticipation to rise
from the fall

SYMBOLISING
THE TRAITS INSIDE

SYMBOLISING
MIRROR OF
REFLECTION

reflecing out exactly similar
whats inside of one

free of deceit and untruthfulness
with sinciere and truthful
attributes

SYMBOLISING A PART

+

SYMBOLISING
MEANINGLESS CLUSTER

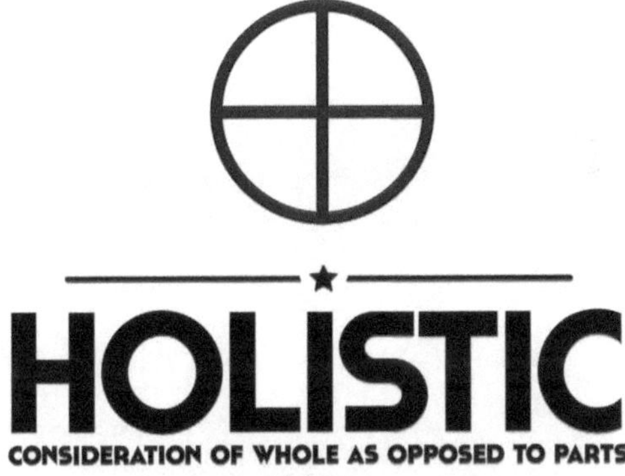

HOLISTIC

CONSIDERATION OF WHOLE AS OPPOSED TO PARTS

percieving the complete shape in
a meaningful fashion as opposed
to viewing it as seperate parts

characterized by the treatment of
the whole person, taking into
account mental and social
factors, rather than just
the physical

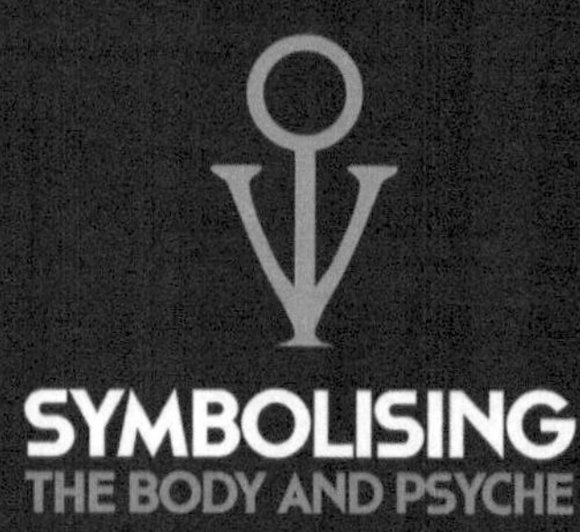

SYMBOLISING
THE BODY AND PSYCHE

SYMBOLISING
THE ENLIGHTENMENT

ILLUMINATION

THE SENSE OF HIGHER INTELECTUAL ENLIGHTENMENT

experiencing the aura of
enlightenment around your mind

the feeling of spiritual and
intellectual enlightenment

SYMBOLISING
THE EVENT TO OCCUR

+

SYMBOLISING
THE PRIOR NOTIFICATION
OF AN EVENT TO OCCUR

INTUTION

MARKED PRIOR TO ACTUAL OCCURENCE OR EXISTENCE

sensing a relative similar
notification of what is about
to happen

★ ★ ★

knowing or considering likely
from inside feeling rather than
conscious reasoning

SYMBOLISING
THE FLOW OF IDEAS
FROM INTUTIVE THINKING

+

SYMBOLISING
THE FLOW OF IDEAS
FROM CONCIOUS THINKING

IMAGINAIVE

PHENOMENON OF EXCEPTIONAL PERCEPTION

the exceptional blend of intutive
and concious thinking
intertwined to result in excellent
sense of perception

★ ★ ★

tendency to showi creativity and
exceptional inventiveness

+

SYMBOLISING
THE UNSURITY
OF DIRECTION

INFATUATION
LOSS OF SENSE OF ENVIRONMENT & DIRECTION

an extravagant passion making
one loose the sense of
its environmetn and direction

★ ★ ★

the state of being infatuated
and foolishness

SYMBOLISING
THE NATURAL STATE

SYMBOLISING
THE RESPONSE
DUE TO THE OCCURENCE OF AN ACTION

INSTINCTIVE

THE OCCURENCE OF THE IMPACT OF NATURAL STIMULI

response apparently unconscious
or automatic due to an occurence
of action causing the natural
state to alter from its original

performing a specified thing
apparently naturally or
automatically

SYMBOLISING
THE IMPARTIALITY
BEING BALANCED

+

SYMBOLISING
PRINCIPLE AND VALUES
GOVERNING THE BALANCE

JUSTICE

BOUND BY FAVOURABLE & IMPARTIAL BALANCE

being impartial and balanced
towards the parties in the
objectivity of making decision

the quality of being fair and
reasonable

SYMBOLISING
THE CONCENTRATED
INTELLECTUALITY

+

SYMBOLISING
THE FRAMEWORK
OF BRAIN

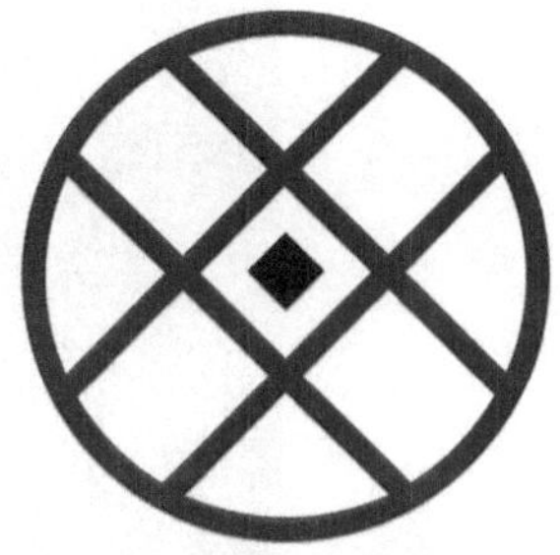

KNOWLEDGE
ABSORBING DEEP WITHIN THE INTELLECT

the absorption of knowledge
absorbed deep within

information and skills acquired
through experience or education

SYMBOLISING
THE CHANCES

+

SYMBOLISING
THE FORTUNATE

opportuntiy striked over the one
against other cahnces

having or bringing good fortune

SYMBOLISING
DIRECTNESS

LACONIC
BEING DIRECT IN ITS ATTRIBUTE

using very few words to be
concise and direct in
its approach

★ ★ ★

brief and to the point; effectively
cut short

SYMBOLISING
THE STATE OF MIND

+

SYMBOLISING
THE STATE OF BODY

LOVE

PHENOMENON OF MAKING ONE FEEL LOST

An intense feeling of deep
affection causing one to loose
its senses

★ ★ ★

the intense feeling of passion
towards someone causing one to
feel messed up in its own

★ ★ ★

SYMBOLISING
THE COMFORT CUSHION

\+

\=

SYMBOLISING
THE STABLE STATE
OF DORMANCY

LUXURY

DORMANT BOUNDED BY THE COMFORT

cushioned comfortably resting
amongst riches

experiencing the state of great
comfort and extravagant living

SYMBOLISING
THE BOUNDARY

SYMBOLISING
FORCING OUT

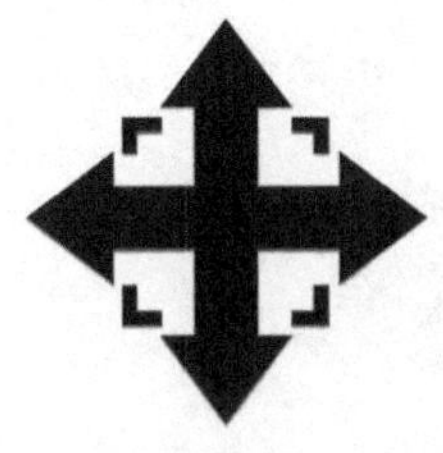

LIBERTY

EXPERIENCING FREEDOM FROM OPRESSION

the phenomenon of outbreaking
the opression to express
oneself free

★ ★ ★

the state of being free within
society from oppressive
restrictions imposed by authority
on one's way of life

SYMBOLISING
A DEEP PSYCHE

+

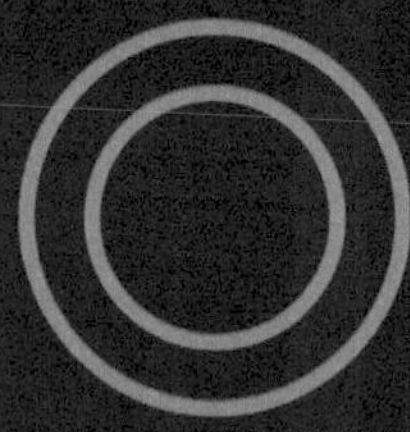

SYMBOLISING
THE CHANNELS
TO ATTAIN THAT STATE

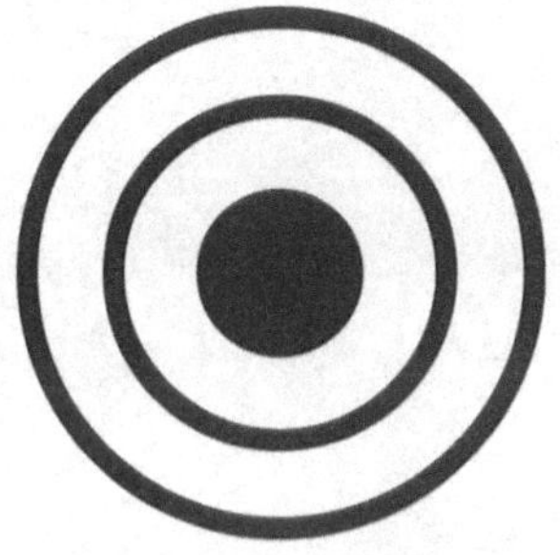

MYSTIC

PHENOMENON BEYOND AND UNKNOWN

the phenomenon of seeking by
contemplation and self-surrender
to obtain unity with the absolute

of or relating to religious
mysteries or occult rites and
practices

**SYMBOLISING
THE UPWARD
RIGHT-HANDED PATH**

**SYMBOLISING
THE DOWNWARD
LEFT HANDED PATH**

MAGIC

CONTROL THROUGH BALANCE OF LEFT & RIGHT HANDED PATH

the art achieving perfect balance
by creating the systematic blend
of positives and negatives

possessing distinctive qualities
by the balance to produce
unaccountable or baffling effects

SYMBOLISING
THE CROWN

+

SYMBOLISING
BOLD ATTIRE
WITH STRENGTH AND POWER

impressively beautiful with
extravagant boldness to be
crowned high

resembling the quality of
power and strength

SYMBOLISING
THE EVENT
PERCIEVED

SYMBOLISING
THE EVENT
REMEMBERED

MEMORY

REPLICATING THE EXACT OCCURENCE INSIDE

the tendency to store and recall
the similar instance at a later
period of time

★ ★ ★

the double helical structure of
DNA tends to carry the hereditry
information and memory

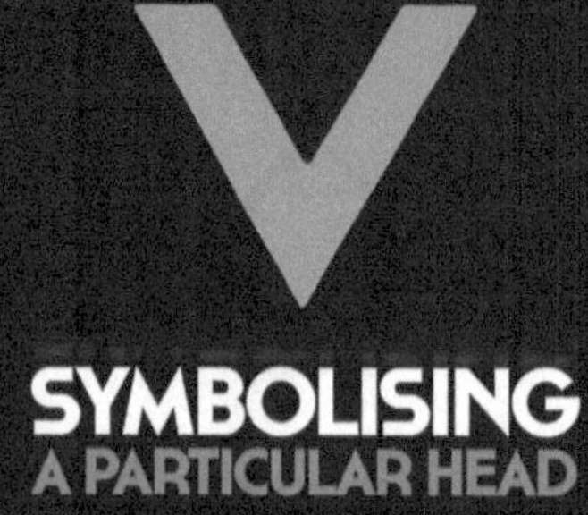

SYMBOLISING
A PARTICULAR HEAD

SYMBOLISING
ANOTHER HEAD

the bond created by equally
nuetral parties to share intrests
and resources with
understanding

action done by each of two or
more parties toward each
other or others

SYMBOLISING
THE FLOW

SYMBOLISING
THE BALANCE OF
HARMONY

the feeling of upliftment beyond
ones comfort zone. the circle
with the prime association of
infinity raised over the balance of

the sun is the resemblance of the
perfection mounted static
crowned denoting the power of
supremacy. Bound by excelence
and infinte existencve it
is never deviated

SYMBOLISING
THE OTHERS RESOURCES

+

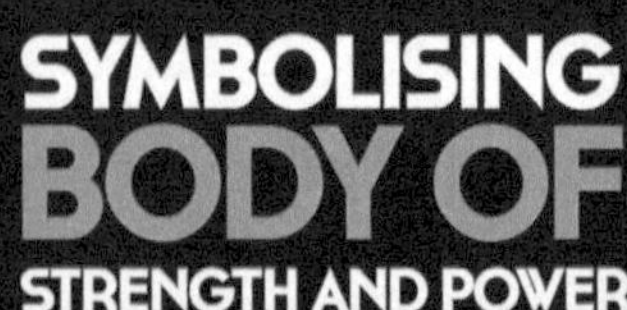
SYMBOLISING
BODY OF
STRENGTH AND POWER

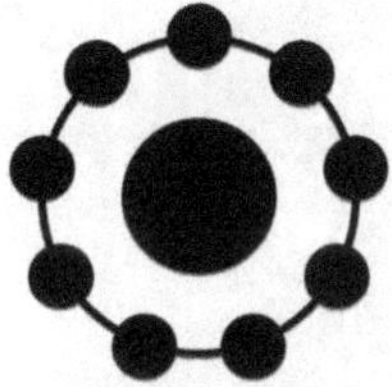

MONOPOLY
THE EXCLUSIVE CONTROL OVER OTHERS

the exclusive possession, control
and exercise of something

★ ★ ★

bound to orbit others around
onself due to the possession of
exclusive power and strength

SYMBOLISING
THE BODY OF
AUTHORITY

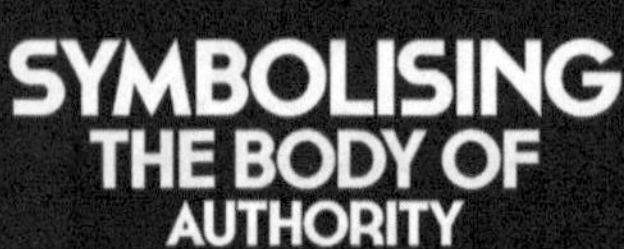

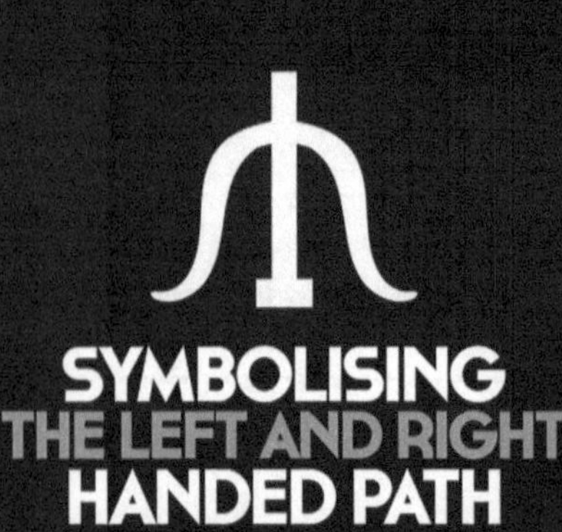

SYMBOLISING
THE LEFT AND RIGHT
HANDED PATH

MORAL

GOVERNED BY THE AUTHORITY OF GOOD & BAD

duty to justify and follow the
obligations of right and
wrong deeds

concerned with the principles of
right and wrong behavior and the
goodness or badness of human
character

SYMBOLISING
THE ORDINARY

+

SYMBOLISING
THE SIMPLICITY

MARVELOUS
BOUND TO BE EXTRA ORDINARY

the simplicity built into
extraordnary inception is bound
to cause great wonder

★ ★ ★

being or having the character
of a miracle

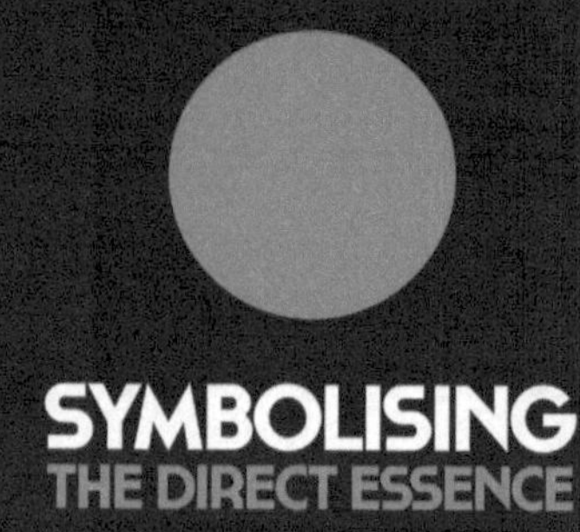
SYMBOLISING
THE DIRECT ESSENCE

NATURAL
SIMPLIFIED IN ITS DIRECT ESSENCE

existing in its most natural form

★ ★ ★

characterized by spontaneity and
freedom from artificiality,
affectation, or inhibitions

SYMBOLISING
ONE DIRECT
PRPORTION

+

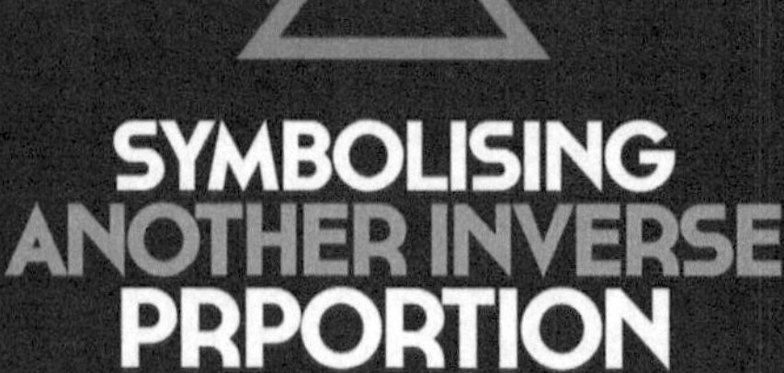

SYMBOLISING
ANOTHER INVERSE
PRPORTION

OPTIMAL
ACHIEVING THE PERFECT BALANCE

creating or choosing the optimal
blend of aspects

most desirable possible under a
restriction expressed or implied

SYMBOLISING OUTWARD FLOW OF ENERGY

SYMBOLISING THE POSITIVE

OPTIMISM

MARKED WITH THE SENSE OF POSITIVITY

directing the flow of energy
outward to achieve with the
positive attitude

the belief that good will
ultimately triumph over evil and
that virtue will be rewarded

SYMBOLISING
THE CROWN
POSSESSION OF POWER

+

SYMBOLISING
THE HEIGHT
AND STABILITY

OMNIPOTENT
CROWNED THE ONE HIGHEST MOST POWERFUL

crowned the one at highest with
greatest of stability

★ ★ ★

having unlimited or universal
power, authority, or force;
all-powerful

★ ★ ★

SYMBOLISING
THE UNIFIED STATE

SYMBOLISING
THE FAVOURABLE
BALANCE

OBJECTIVE

INTENTION TARGETED WITH UNBIASEDNESS

uninfluenced by emotions or
personal prejudices being
in position of balanced
decision making

being equal in both
the directions

SYMBOLISING
THE FORCE

+

SYMBOLISING
THE BEARER

PATIENCE

POTENTIAL TO RESIST FORCE FOR LONG

ability to resist or being in
particualr state for long

potential to wait for the event to
occur and let the sand flow

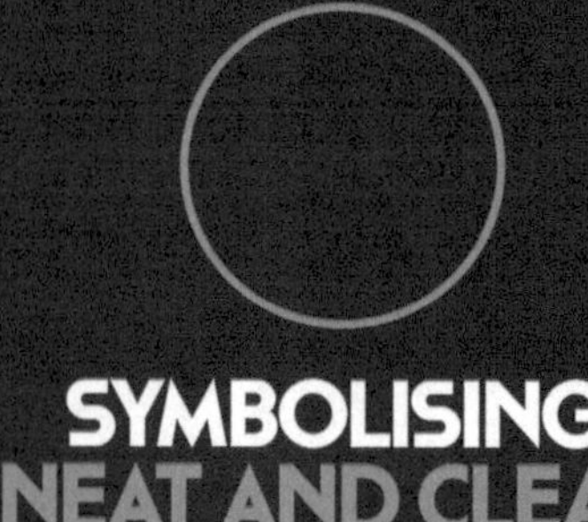
SYMBOLISING
NEAT AND CLEAN

the quality or condition of being
simple, clean cand clear

the one innocently perceived
with no embellishment
and extravagance

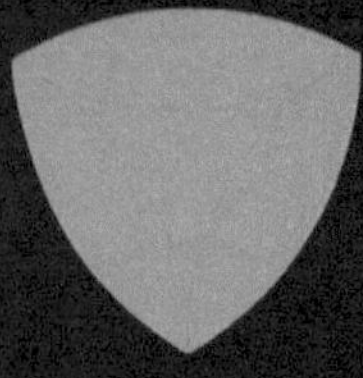

SYMBOLISING
THE SHILEDED PRINCIPLES
OF WISDOM AND EXISTENCE

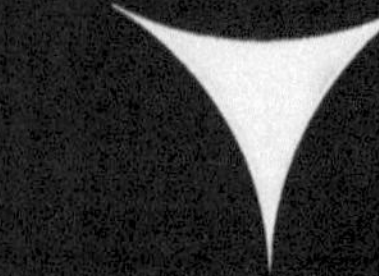

SYMBOLISING
THE DISPERSION

PHILOSOPHY

EXPANDING OVER THE FUNDAMENTALS OF EXISTENCE

dispersian over the unknown
shielded truth of life
and existence

★ ★ ★

love and pursuit of attaining
wisdom by intellectual means
and moral self-discipline to
discover and realize the truths

SYMBOLISING
THE STORED ENERGY
IN A FREE PENDULUM

SYMBOLISING
THE DISPERSION
OF POTENTIAL ENERGY

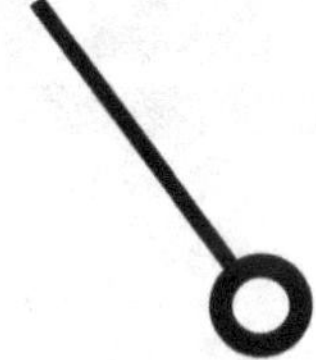

POTENTIAL
POSSESSING THE FORCE TO MOVE

possessing the ability and
resources to bring or
cause changes

★ ★ ★

capable of being but not
yet in existence

 ★ ★ ★

SYMBOLISING
THE STABILE AUTHORITY
OF PERFECTION AND BALANCE

SYMBOLISING
THE DEDICATED
DEVOTION

PIOUS

EXHIBITING STABLE DEDICATED DEVOTION

being bound to show devotion for
a powerful authority

★ ★ ★

having or showing a dutiful
spirit of reverence for God
or hindered

———————— ★ ★ ★ ————————

SYMBOLISING
THE ACTION AS TO HAPPEN
ON A STIPULATED TIME

+

**SYMBOLISING
THE OCCURENCE
OF THE ACTION**

PUNCTUAL

PRECISE TO THE ANTICIPATED OCCURENCE

occurence of the action or event
similarly as stipulated or planned

★ ★ ★

arriving or taking place at an
arranged time

SYMBOLISING
THE ACT OR OBJECT

+

SYMBOLISING
THE BALANCE OF
AUTHORITY AND PERFECTION

★
PERMANENT
EMBEDED DEEP WITHIN THE CORE

something embeded so intense to
the core making it presence felt
for an endless time

★ ★ ★

not expected to change for an
indefinite time

★ ★ ★

SYMBOLISING
THE INCLINATION

+

SYMBOLISING
THE NATION

PATRIOTIC

INCLINATION TOWARDS NATION

the feeling of favour and
devotion towards one's nation

love of country and willingness
to sacrifice for it

+

SYMBOLISING
PERCEPTION
AND RESPONSE

QUICK

the instance of an action
traversing a swift-second path
from initial to terminal point

Perceiving or responding with
speed and sensitivity

SYMBOLISING
THE ELEMENT

+

SYMBOLISING
THE RESTORATION

RESURECTION
REVIVAL OF THE ONCE GONE

the restoration of once that
happened previously into the
same state of existence

the act of bringing back bounded
by the cycle of infinite existence
taking place again and again

SYMBOLISING
THE FEMININE ASPECT

+

SYMBOLISING
THE MASCULINE ASPECT

ROMANTIC
FREE FLOW OF EMOTIONS TOWARDS LOVE

the flow of emotions cherished
between two

★ ★ ★

an intense and happy lived affair
involving young people

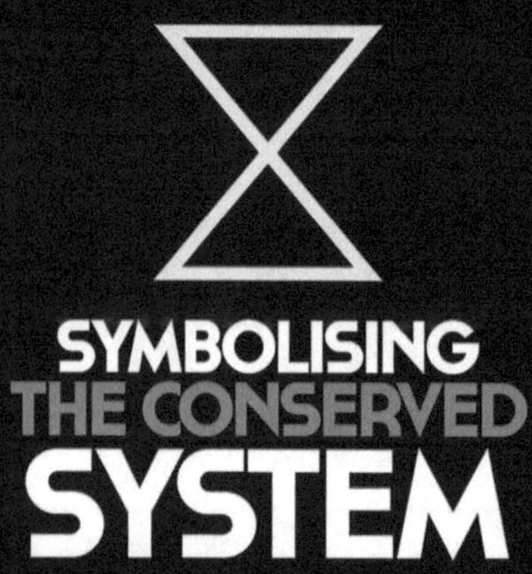
SYMBOLISING
THE CONSERVED
SYSTEM

SYMBOLISING
THE INITIATIVE
TO CHALLANGE

REVOLUTION
OUTBREAKING FOR A CHANGE

outbreak and overthrow of the
constructed systems and bounds

a complete and forcible
overthrow and replacement of
an established government or
political system by the
people governed

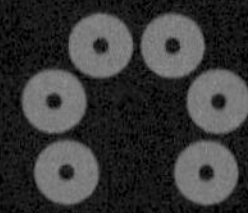

SYMBOLISING
THE STATES PRIOR
AND LATER

SYMBOLISING
THE AURA

REJUVENATION
PHENOMENON OF VITALITY BEING RESTORED

the process of restoring the
youthful vigor or appearance

the phenomenon of vitality and
freshness being restored

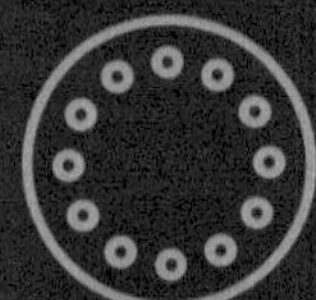

SYMBOLISING
THE ECSTACY INSIDE

+

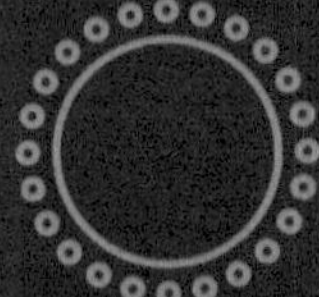

SYMBOLISING
FLOWING OUT

RAPTURE
THE OUTBURST OF THE EMOTIONS INSIDE OUT

the outflow of feelings
stored inside out

★ ★ ★

the feeling of intense pleasure
demonstrating the feelings out

SYMBOLISING
AN EVENT OR ACTION

+

SYMBOLISING
THE CYCLE

the phenomenon of systematic
repitition and occurence of
an event or action

★ ★ ★

occurring with normal or healthy
frequency

★ ★ ★

SYMBOLISING
A PARTICULAR FORM
+
SYMBOLISING
ITS REPLICATION

to form, construct, or create
anew from similar

the ability or tendency to grow
seperately or simultaneously
as a new part, similar or
advanced in nature

SYMBOLISING
THE BODY AT REST

\+

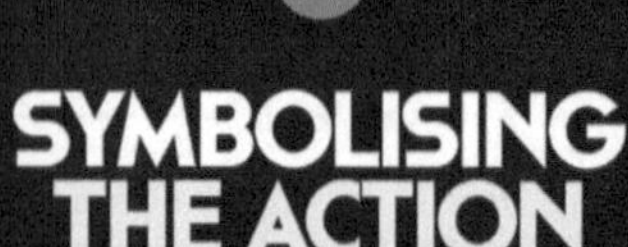

SYMBOLISING
THE ACTION

the occuring stimuli for a
certain action

★ ★ ★

a tendency causing to revert
to a former state

★ ★ ★

SYMBOLISING
THE USUAL

+

SYMBOLISING
THE FAVOURED

SPECIAL
EXISTENCE FAVORED HIGHER THAN USUAL

one treated distinctly than others

★ ★ ★

distinct among others of a kind

★ ★ ★

SYMBOLISING
THE PLANE

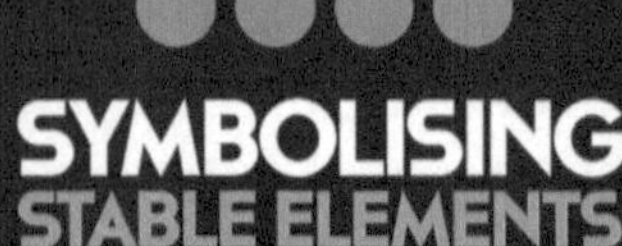

SYMBOLISING
STABLE ELEMENTS

the state of being grounded at
their positions without any
noticeable disturbance or motion

the condition or quality of
being or keeping still

SYMBOLISING
UNDECEITFUL

SINCIERE
STRAIGHT AND CLEAN IN ITS APPROACH

characterised by non deceitful
and clean attributes

★ ★ ★

characterized by an inability to
mask the attributes

SYMBOLISING
THE STATE OF EMOTION

+

SYMBOLISING
ACQUIRED FRAME

SATISFACTION

CONTENDED WITHIN THE ACQUIRED LIMITS

in a tendency of being stable
with no intention to rise or
move further

★ ★ ★

the contentment derived from
the fulfillment or gratification
of a desire

SYMBOLISING
THE TENDENCY

SYMBOLISING
THE LIMIT

TRANSCEND
GOING BEYOND THE LIMITS

the tendancy to go beyond the
marked limits

★ ★ ★

to rise above or go beyond the
ordinary limits of excellence

I

SYMBOLISING
THE ONLY ONE

UNIQUE

being the only one standing
unchallanged in its own aura
unparalled by any other

★ ★ ★

being the only one of a particular
type leading to only one result

★ ★ ★

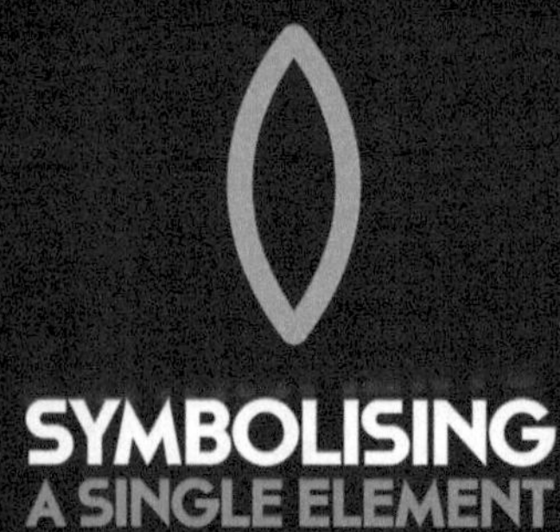

SYMBOLISING
A SINGLE ELEMENT

\+

SYMBOLISING
THE BOND

UNITED

BONDED TOGETHER BY A COMMON CAUSE

joining hands together for a
mutual relationship or benefit

★ ★ ★

made into or caused to act as
a single entity

**SYMBOLISING
THE STABILITY**

+

**SYMBOLISING
DEFEATING**

VICTORIOUS

CHARACTERISED BY THE TRIUMPH OF HIGHNESS

standing successfull in a struggle
against difficulties or an obstacle

★ ★ ★

a triumph over an enemy in
battle or war

 ★ ★ ★

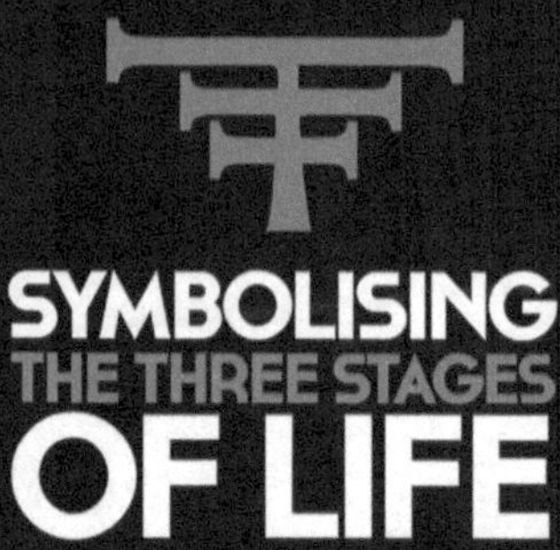

SYMBOLISING
THE THREE STAGES
OF LIFE

SYMBOLISING
THE CROWN OF
ACHIEVEMENT

crowned with its ability of right
and just decision making learned
through experience

the ability or result of an ability
to think and act utilizing
knowledge, experience,
understanding, common sense,
and insight

SYMBOLISING
AN ELEGANT PETAL

+

SYMBOLISING
THE STRENGTHENED
SYMMETERY

WONDERFUL
PERFECTLY BALANCED TO BE ADMIRED

with a perfect blend of curves
and balanced symmetry that of
flower of lilly to be admired

excellently trewated with
grand admiration

SYMBOLISING
QUICK CHANNEL
OF STIMULI

+

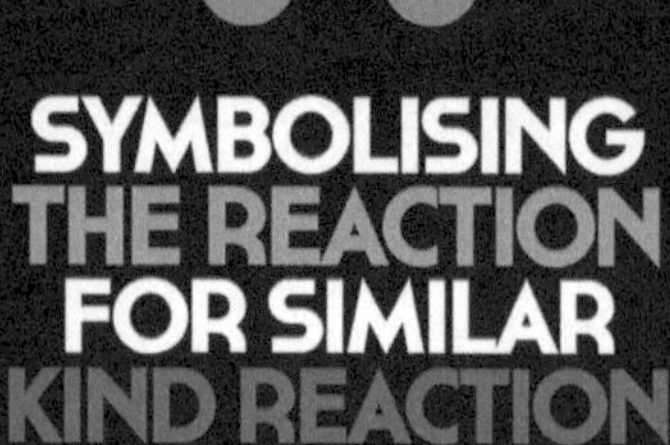

SYMBOLISING
THE REACTION
FOR SIMILAR
KIND REACTION

WITTY

the quick and clever response
for the action performed
simultaneously

★ ★ ★

amusingly fast and clever in
perception and expression

★ ★ ★

SYMBOLISING
AN ENDLESS
ROUTE

WANDERLUST
A DESIRE TO TRAVEL ENDLESSLY

a very strong or irresistible
impulse to travel

★ ★ ★

getting immensely lost
in traveling

SYMBOLISING
HARDENED STRENGTH

+

SYMBOLISING
THE STABILITY

attaining a toughned and bold
form difficult to be challenged

depicting the muscular strength
and the stablity in its form,
standing hardned and tough

SYMBOLISING
THE FREE CONCENTRATED
PARTICLES

+

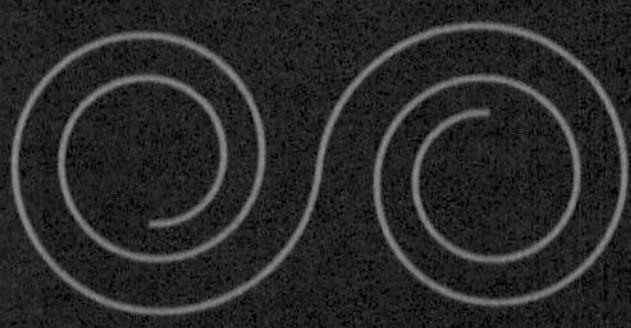

SYMBOLISING
THE FREE FLOW

XENON

FREEDOM OF FLOWING FREE WITHOUT BOUNDATION

the ability to disperse oneself
and flow with freedom

a unique ability to blend and
mould with flow in any situation

SYMBOLISING
DIRECTION OF GROWTH

+

SYMBOLISING
CONCENTRATED ENERGY

fueled with the concentrated
potential to move towards
growth and progress

in a stage of tendency to
progress and develop

SYMBOLISING
THE FREE SPIRIT

expression created from a spirit
free from the influences
experiencing the freedom
of mind

practice of exclusion of all else
so to achieve pure enlightenment
creating an expression

SYMBOLISING
THE FLOW OF ENERGY

+

SYMBOLISING
THE PROGRESSION
OF ENERGY

the process of building in the
energy concentrated to be
leashed out

filled with or inspired by intense
enthusiasm or energy

Its about perceiving the world from a distinct eye, causing to find meaning that lies hidden deep into the essence of an element. The art of perceiving other ways, is only responsible for new discoveries and inventions helping us to understand the inherit character of any essence. This is a little effort made to demonstrate and guide how one can look at things from another angle.

T H Ξ W

Signerika embarks you over a journey of subliminal discovery of self by decoding metaphors and visuals appearing mundane but contain the deepest secrets to unveil.

Unleashing your inner magic and desire to craft your own reality, it unfathoms the workings of the subconscious and how it transforms visions into reality. With progression, Signerika enables you to understand and master the power you can use to create your own world.

Further it makes a perfect artefact for it beautiful pages balanced with fineness and minimalism where reader can pick and start from anywhere to dwell into the mysteries of iconic secrecy.

This is not:
A rule Book. It invites you to construct your own rule and put forward your own Justifcation.
The collection of logos, symbols or branding guide.

This is:
A tool empowering the reader with a sense to discover hidden meanings around.
The compilations of Ideas enlivened as forms.
An allegory demonstarting how simple construct can be made to manifest as a profound interpretation.

It can aid one in creating logos, mascots, symbols, notions, icons, infographics, emblems or an expression of art ready to be framed.

Its ideal to start from begining to end but not mandatory in case of Signerika as each page in itslef transcripts an information that can be experienced in its imperennial solitude.

Signerika is about perceiving the world from a distinct eye and unraveling meaning that lies hidden deep into the essence of an element. The art of looking sideways, is only responsible for new discoveries and inventions helping us to understand the inherit charcter of any essence.

This is a path which demonstrates and guides, how one can look from other perspective.

Bon Voyage!

Ω R M S

www.ingramcontent.com/pod-product-compliance
Lightning Source LLC
Chambersburg PA
CBHW051247250726
48656CB00004B/1175